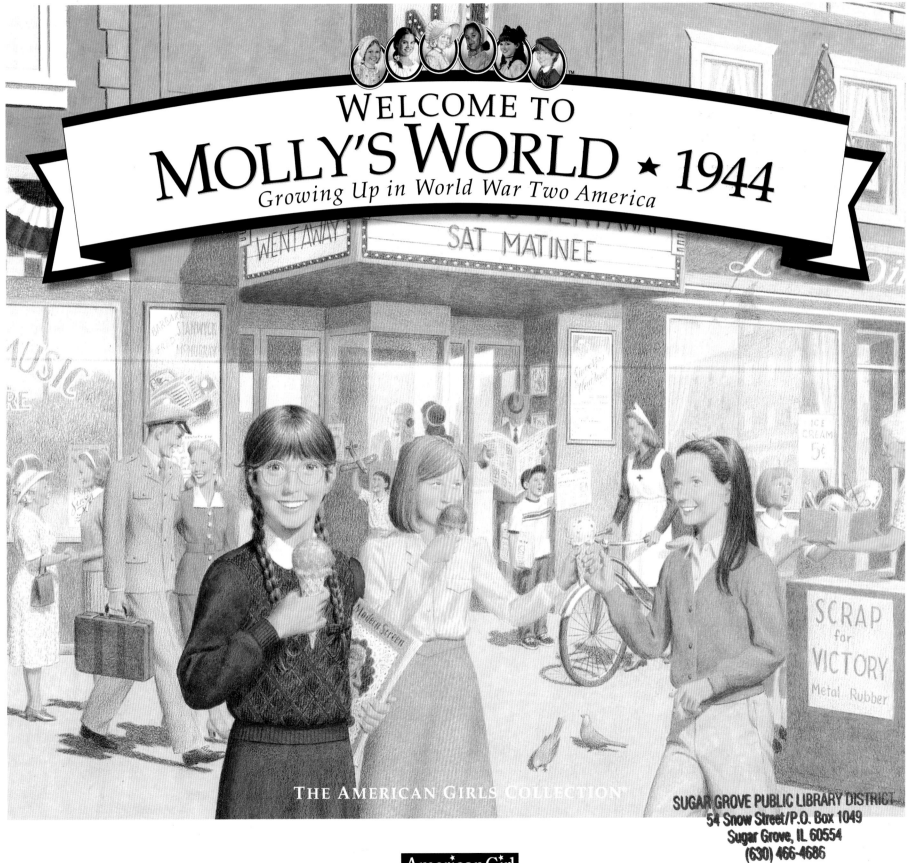

WELCOME TO
MOLLY'S WORLD ★ 1944
Growing Up in World War Two America

WENT AWAY SAT MATINEE

SCRAP for VICTORY Metal Rubber

ICE CREAM 5¢

THE AMERICAN GIRLS COLLECTION

American Girl

Printed in Singapore
99 00 01 02 03 04 05 TWP 10 9 8 7 6 5 4 3 2 1
The American Girls Collection®, Molly®, Molly McIntire®, and the
American Girl logo are trademarks of Pleasant Company.

Written by Catherine Gourley
Edited by Camela Decaire and Jodi Evert
Historical and Editorial Consulting by American Historical Publications
Designed and Art Directed by Mengwan Lin, Ingrid Slamer, and Jane S. Varda
Produced by Lori Armstrong, Cheryll Mellenthin, and Paula Moon
Cover Illustration by Nick Backes
Interior Illustrations by Laszlo Kubinyi, Susan McAliley, Susan Moore, and Jean-Paul Tibbles
Illustration Research by Rebecca Sample Bernstein, Andy Kraushaar
Photo Research by Sally Jacobs, Andy Kraushaar
Photography by Jamie Young, Connie Russell
Prop Research and Styling by Jean doPico

Library of Congress Cataloging-in-Publication Data
Welcome to Molly's world, 1944 — growing up in World War Two America /
[written by Catherine Gourley; edited by Camela Decaire and Jodi Evert;
designed by Ingrid Slamer and Jane S. Varda; photography by Jamie Young].
p. cm. — (The American girls collection)
Summary: Provides an in-depth look at life and historical events
in America during World War Two.
ISBN 1-56247-773-0
1. World War, 1939-1945—United States—Juvenile literature.
I. Gourley, Catherine, 1950—   II. Kubinyi, Laszlo   III. Title   IV. Series
D769.G68 1999 940.53'73—dc21 99–27622 CIP AC

Table of Contents

Welcome to Molly's World

When a letter came from Dad, everyone gathered while Mrs. McIntire read it aloud. Even though Dad's letters were long and funny and wonderful, they still sounded as if they came from very far away.

—Meet Molly

★

I n 1944, when Molly was nine years old, America had been fighting in World War Two for three years. During the war, Molly learned to make do with less. She ate foods she didn't like, such as mashed turnips. She worked with the other girls in her class to collect much-needed scrap paper and metal for the war effort. Molly also tried to be understanding of Emily Bennett, the girl who had come from war-torn England to live with the McIntires. Every day, though, Molly wished the war had never happened. The hardest thing, of course, was missing her father. If there had never been a war, then he would never have gone away.

Around her neck, Molly wore a heart-shaped locket. Inside was a picture of her father. Whenever Molly clicked open the locket, Dr. McIntire was always smiling back at her, giving her the courage and confidence to do the right thing.

Molly McIntire is a fictional character. But the place and the time of her story are real. In fact, all the characters in Molly's world are drawn from memories, letters, and diaries of real girls and women, soldiers and civilians from the 1940s. The war changed their lives and America forever.

In this book, you will travel back in time and read about the choices and challenges that girls like Molly faced, both on the American home front and on the battle front overseas. You will meet real people and learn what their lives were like during wartime. The journey to Molly's world begins as most journeys do . . . with a map.

A World at War

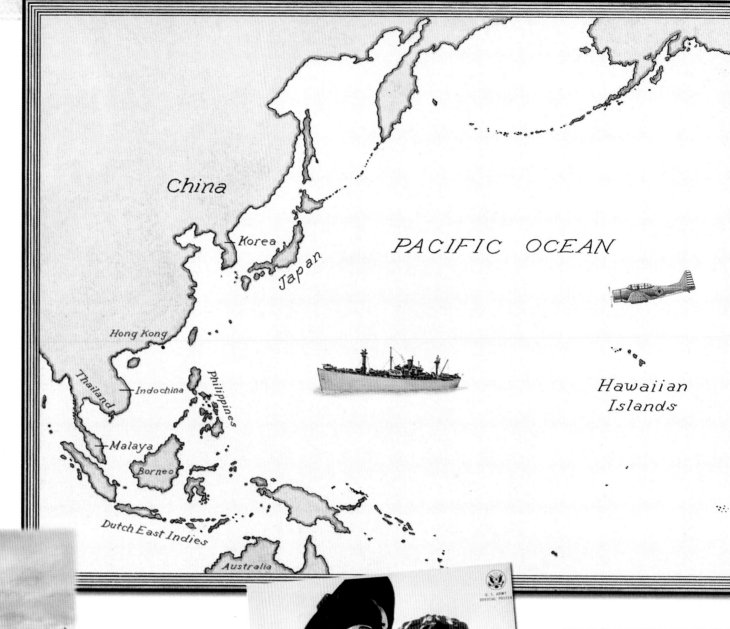

A map of the world hung on the wall of Molly's classroom. Like students all across the United States, Molly studied the map and learned about a world at war. American troops were fighting against Japan on islands in the South Pacific Ocean. They were also fighting against Germany and Italy in Europe and in Africa. At home, Americans were full of hope that peace would come soon. But until then, everyone did whatever they could to support the war effort.

China

Korea

Japan

PACIFIC OCEAN

Hong Kong

Thailand

Indochina

Philippines

Malaya

Borneo

Hawaiian Islands

Dutch East Indies

Australia

①　SAN FRANCISCO
Battleships carrying thousands of soldiers left San Francisco daily, heading for the war in the South Pacific. For the troops on board, the Golden Gate Bridge was the last sight of America.

②　FACTORIES AND SHIPYARDS
When men left for war, thousands of women went to work in factories and war plants. They made ships and airplanes, bullets and parachutes.

SOLDIERS *without guns*

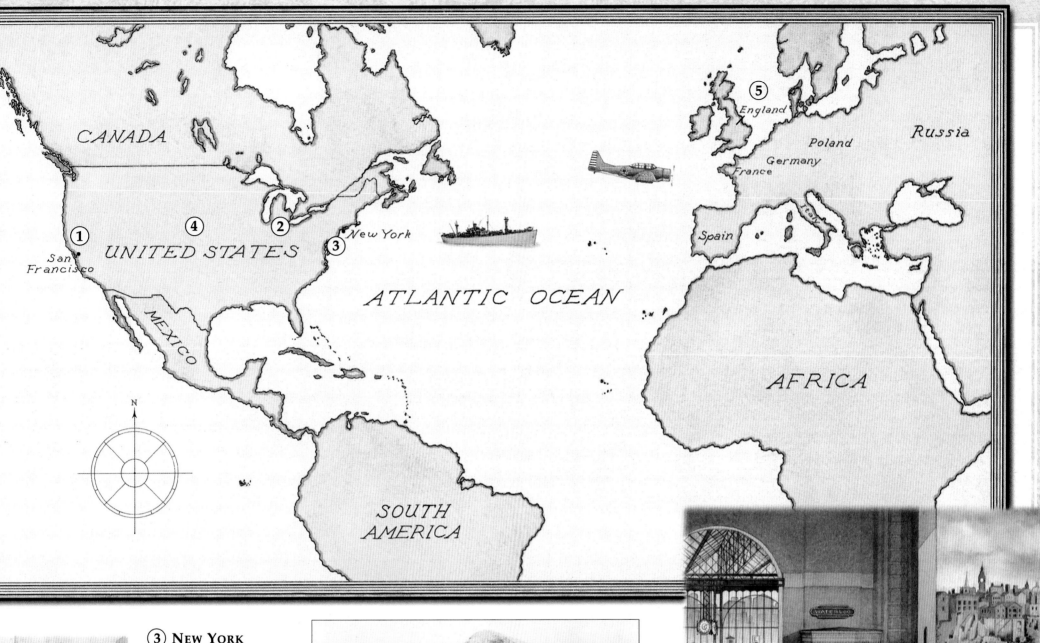

CANADA

UNITED STATES

San Francisco

MEXICO

① ④ ②

③ New York

ATLANTIC OCEAN

SOUTH AMERICA

England ⑤

Poland

Germany

France

Spain

Italy

Russia

AFRICA

N

③ New York Harbor
Red Cross volunteers—called "gray ladies" because of their uniforms—served coffee and doughnuts to soldiers about to ship out for the war front. Many soldiers would never return.

④ Farmland
Women helped keep farms running to produce America's food. But gasoline and machine parts were scarce. They were needed for tanks and jeeps, too.

⑤ London, England
American troops arrived in London by the thousands in 1944. America and England were loyal *allies*. Along with Soviet Russia, they fought together against Japan, Germany, and Italy.

False Promises

Molly could point to the places on the world map where American soldiers were fighting. She could even tell who they were fighting—the people of Japan, Germany, and Italy. But why was the world at war? The map didn't answer that question. Miss Campbell might have explained it this way: In the 1930s, people in many countries around the world were suffering. They had no jobs, no food, and no money. In Germany, a man named Adolf Hitler promised jobs and food to eat. But once Hitler took control, he became a cruel *dictator*, or someone who rules without having to answer to anyone.

YELLOW STAR OF DAVID
As a dictator, Hitler preached that some people were better than others. He particularly looked down on Jewish people. He forced them to wear the Yellow Star of David, a symbol of their religion, sewn onto their clothing.

*The Nazi symbol was a **swastika**. It was once a symbol of good luck, but became a symbol of hatred and horror.*

ADOLF HITLER
Adolf Hitler vowed to build Germany into a strong nation. But his ideas encouraged hatred. Thousands of followers, called *Nazis*, cheered Hitler. But many other Germans were afraid of the dictator's power.

The three dictators slice up a watermelon world to share.

DICTATORS
Hitler was not the only dictator in the world. Mussolini ruled Italy and Emperor Hirohito ruled Japan. All three dictators joined together, forming the *Axis powers*. They planned to conquer the world.

BEATEN
France and Britain had promised to help Poland. Now they became Hitler's main targets. After defeating the French Army, Hitler marched right into Paris. Soon German planes began bombing Britain.

THE ROUNDUP
In time, Hitler began to arrest Jewish people. Soldiers forced them into camps and crowded neighborhoods called *ghettos*. Those who tried to escape were shot.

HITLER INVADES POLAND
Hitler wanted to rule all of Europe, not just Germany. In September 1939, he sent Nazi troops into Poland. "Be brutal," he commanded. In less than a week, Poland surrendered.

The Polish army never had a chance. Soldiers on horses were helpless against Hitler's tanks.

MOTHERS WILL NOT LEND or LEASE THEIR SONS

KEEP U.S. OUT OF WAR BE NEUTRAL

AMERICANS DISAGREE
Some Americans wanted to fight the Axis powers. But others thought America should stay out of war. After all, two large oceans protected America from invasion. Then, a surprise attack on an American naval base changed everything.

Some parents especially hoped America would stay out of war. They feared for their children.

It's War!

On Sunday, December 7, 1941, Japanese bombers attacked Pearl Harbor, the site of an American naval base in Hawaii. The attack was just one part of a Japanese plan to create an empire in the South Pacific.

The tiny islands that made up Japan were crowded with more than 80 million people. Their army had begun to seize land in countries all around Japan. To force Japan to stop, America held back all shipments of basic supplies, such as oil, to the country. Japan responded by destroying the U.S. base at Pearl Harbor.

TELEGRAM
It was 2:00 P.M. in Washington, D.C. President Roosevelt was relaxing after lunch when the phone rang. The head of the navy had just received a very serious telegram.

U. S. S. RANGER
NAVAL DISPATCH

Heading: NSS NR 977 Z ØF8 2B 3Ø ØF3 ØF4 Ø BT

AIR RAID ON PEARL HARBOR X THIS IS NOT DRILL

EXECUTIVE   Date 7 DEC 41 ED

From: CINCPAC
To: CINCLA NT COMAF OPNAV   No. 33

Info:

ACTION
INFO

ATTACK!
The Japanese attack on Pearl Harbor lasted less than two hours. But it destroyed most of the base's warships and killed more than 2,000 people.

State Edition   THE CHICAGO DAI
66TH YEAR—288.   MONDAY, DECEMBER 8, 1941—TWENTY-EIG

IT'S WAR!
BOMB HA

350 Yanks Slain; | BRITISH TO ACT; | A United Nation
Guam Is Bombed | PARLIAMENT IN | SPECIAL SESSION
                | WAR BULLETINS.

FEAR
Immediately after the attack, soldiers covered Hawaii's beautiful beaches with rolls of barbed wire. The wire would slow down Japanese soldiers in case of an invasion.

HEADLINES
Most Americans heard of the Japanese attack over the radio or through newspapers. Within days, the news was worse. Japan's allies, Germany and Italy, also declared war on America.

CONQUEST
Japanese soldiers attacked and conquered more islands in the South Pacific Ocean. By midsummer, it looked as though Japan might even attack Australia.

Shipping Out

Within a year, thousands of soldiers left America for battle fronts. They traveled on troopships. One of the largest ships was the *Queen Mary*. Before the war, this luxury ocean liner had elegant parlors, a grand ballroom, a library, and even playrooms for children. During the war, the British government removed the ship's carpets and crystal chandeliers, its gold-framed paintings and sculptures. Workers painted the hull gray and mounted machine guns and rocket launchers on the decks. At the height of the war, the *Queen* could transport as many as 15,000 soldiers.

③ FROM PLAY TO WORK
The on-ship office of the British Royal Air Force was once a children's playroom.

④ *Only officers were allowed in the main lounge, the one room that had not been stripped of its furnishings. But even this room was dark and gloomy. All its windows were blacked out so enemy ships could not see the* **Queen Mary** *at night.*

KEEP THIS CARD
In order to supply all the soldiers on board the ship with a bed, shower, and two meals a day, the ship was divided into three sections. Soldiers were issued cards that told them when and where to eat, sleep, and work.

② *Rooms that had held two pleasure passengers held as many as 18 bunks for soldiers during wartime.*

① *As a luxury liner, the* **Queen Mary** *boasted the largest main restaurant of any cruise ship and a games deck equal to a football field!*

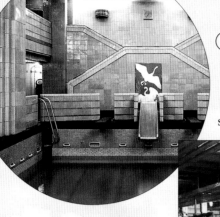

6 **SWIMMING IN BUNKS**
Every possible space on the ship held bunks—even the swimming pool was drained and stacked with bunks seven high! Even so, soldiers still had to share beds and take turns sleeping.

8 **NO MORE GAMES**
In drills, soldiers ran to battle stations. They manned antiaircraft guns on what was once the games deck.

5 *The **Queen Mary's** three **funnels**, or smokestacks, went from glossy red to dull gray during the war so she would be hard to spot on the horizon. Hitler called the ship the "Gray Ghost."*

7 *Troops ate two meals a day. There weren't enough tables and chairs, so they ate standing up.*

9 *Hitler offered a reward of $250,000 to any German submarine that sank the "Gray Ghost." But she was the fastest ship on the seas. She was never caught.*

QUEEN MARY

A Fireside Chat

President Roosevelt often spoke to the American people over the radio. The president called his radio speeches "fireside chats" because he liked to imagine that everyone listening was sitting in a room with him around a fire crackling in the fireplace. On the evening of February 23, 1942, millions of Americans sat in their parlors listening to their radios, anxious to hear what the president would tell them about the war against Germany, Italy, and Japan.

A few days earlier, newspapers had reported that the president wanted his listeners to have a map of the world spread out before them as he spoke. "I am going to talk about strange places that many of them have never heard of—places that are now the battleground for civilization," the president had said. Within days, families all across America had bought maps. Some people tacked them on the wall above their radios.

The president's chat began at 10:00 at night. He told the American people that he believed they could "hear the worst without flinching or losing heart." This war was a new kind of war, he continued, unlike any that Americans had ever fought before. Americans would fight on every continent, every island, and every sea.

Brave men were already fighting battles on the war front, the president said. But their sacrifice wasn't enough. All Americans—women and children, too—had to join the fight on another battle line: the home front. The president told his listeners that within the next year, Americans would build 60,000 airplanes, 45,000 tanks, and 20,000 antiaircraft guns.

The numbers were staggering! Newspaper reporters began to scribble in their notebooks. Why, that meant Americans had to build a plane every four minutes, a tank every seven minutes, and two seagoing ships a day! Could it be done?

Yes! said Roosevelt. He compared the crisis with the terrible struggle Americans had faced more than 150 years earlier in the Revolutionary War. Fearful men had said America could never win independence from England. But American Patriots had proven them wrong.

The days ahead will not be easy, the president warned his radio listeners, but we will prove the fearful wrong again. Victory will be ours!

Even Fala, the president's Scottish terrier, listened to his master's fireside chat.

11

Patriotic Fever at Home

The president's fireside chat was a great success. Some people thought it was the best speech the president had ever made. Patriotic fever swept the country. In homes all across the United States, families followed the president's advice to use it up, wear it out, make it do, or do without.

(1) EXTRA BLANKETS
House thermostats were set no higher than 65 degrees in order to save heating fuel.

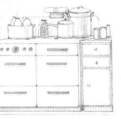

(2) CLOCK
People kept daylight saving time all year round. The additional daylight saved electricity because people used fewer lights.

(3) FOOD RATIONING
Many food items like sugar, meat, and butter became scarce on the home front because soldiers needed them overseas. The government issued food ration stamps to make sure food was distributed fairly. Women carefully sorted and traded their stamps to get what they needed.

(4) CANNED VEGETABLES
Vegetables picked from Victory gardens were boiled or stewed on the stove, then sealed in glass jars for use throughout the winter.

(5) VICTORY GARDEN
For extra food, families planted Victory gardens wherever they had some extra space: in the backyard, along the driveway, or even in a window box.

⑥ UNIFORM
During the war, mothers rose early and dressed for work in factories, offices, or Red Cross centers.

⑦ RADIO
The radio was the center of news and entertainment for 1940s families. There was no television.

⑧ BLACKOUT CURTAINS
In case of an *air-raid*, or enemy attack from the sky, families were prepared to "black out" their windows with heavy cloth so no light could be seen by an enemy plane.

⑨ TELEPHONE
The telephone company asked families not to use phones in the evening. They wanted phone lines left open so men and women in the military could make calls.

⑩ MENDING
Rather than buying new clothes, everyone learned to mend or change what they already had to make it last.

⑪ AIR-RAID SUPPLIES
Families kept air-raid supplies in the basement, including blankets, candles and matches, jugs of water, cans of food, a shovel, and sometimes even a cot.

⑫ MODEL AIRCRAFT
Boys and girls built 500,000 model airplanes that were used to train "spotters" to recognize the differences between American and enemy planes.

Victory Style

Making do meant making way for new fashions, too. The government needed 64 million shirts, 164 million coats, and 229 million pairs of pants for soldiers' uniforms. Cotton and wool material could not be wasted on civilian clothes, so there were no more frilly ruffles or poufy skirts. Instead, Americans invented all-new styles of clothing to help the nation win the war.

PATRIOTIC BEADS AND BANGLES
Girls wore rhinestone pins in the shape of a *V* for victory. And the president's Scottie dog, Fala, inspired all kinds of jewelry!

JOIN THE ARMY
Children wanted to dress in uniforms just as their fathers did overseas.

*Round collars, called **Peter Pan collars**, were popular for girls. They were styled after a costume worn by actress Maude Adams in the play **Peter Pan**.*

SEPARATES
Girls wore *separates*, or blouses and sweaters they could mix with different skirts or jumpers. Girls could make many outfits out of just a few clothes.

A law was passed limiting the amount of fabric that could be used in sleeves and hems.

BOBBY SOCKS
Girls wore bobby socks, which used much less material than tights. The term *bobby socks* came from the word *bob*, which means to shorten.

The straps on jumpers were extra long so they could be adjusted as a girl grew.

UNIFORM CHANGE
Before the war, Girl Scout uniforms had long zippers down the front. Since metal was needed for the war effort, the uniform was redesigned with buttons.

SADDLE SHOES
Saddle shoes were first popular in the 1920s as golf shoes. By the '40s, girls and boys wore them for both work and play.

DICKEYS

Removable collars called *dickeys* were worn instead of blouses under sweaters to save material.

SEW, SAVE, AND SERVE FOR VICTORY

Women remade old clothes into new styles. There were patterns for turning a tablecloth into a new dress.

Rickrack was a popular trim during World War Two, especially in "Flag Red" and "Victory Blue."

SHORT SKIRTS

Hems were let down as many times as possible. Then skirt lengths simply got shorter!

SHOCKING!

The most shocking new style of all was the two-piece bathing suit, which used less fabric than the more modest one-piece suit popular before the war.

This girl is tanning uniform stripes right onto her arm!

WOMEN IN PANTS

Women first wore pants to work in factories. But soon they became acceptable, and even glamorous, everyday wear.

FALLING UNDERWEAR

To save on rubber, underpants were sometimes made with ties rather than elastic waists. If the ties came loose, the underpants fell down!

FAKING IT

Silk and nylon were used to make parachutes, so during the war, there was none to spare for ladies' stockings. Women used leg makeup instead!

Playtime in Wartime

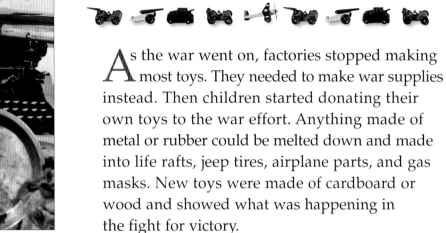

As the war went on, factories stopped making most toys. They needed to make war supplies instead. Then children started donating their own toys to the war effort. Anything made of metal or rubber could be melted down and made into life rafts, jeep tires, airplane parts, and gas masks. New toys were made of cardboard or wood and showed what was happening in the fight for victory.

WARTIME SACRIFICES
This girl gave up her old toys in a *scrap drive*. In scrap drives, children collected old pots, pans, foil, and cans and gave them to a collection center to be made into war equipment.

WATCH JOE GO!
This soldier jumped out of his jeep and into action when wound up. But a girl like Molly would have given him up. He's made of metal.

BANKS
Instead of piggy banks, children used banks shaped like tanks, ships, or the world. Each came with directions to use any saved money to buy war stamps and bonds.

World banks showed where troops were fighting.

PAPER DOLLS
Paper dolls no longer dressed in glamorous evening gowns. They wore the uniforms of Red Cross workers, army nurses, marines, and more.

MIDGIES
These miniature wooden toys came
in an "army camp scene" set for just 98 cents.
None of them was more than three
inches long or tall.

*Even pencil sharpeners
went to war!*

**FIGHTERS
FOR FREEDOM**
War adventure series had
girls and boys dreaming
of the day they would
be old enough to join
the army or navy.

**LITTLE
ORPHAN
ANNIE**
Girls had their own
comic-book heroes.
Fifteen thousand
children joined the
Little Orphan Annie
Junior Commandos.
Annie encouraged
members to win the
war by gathering scrap.

VICTORY GARDEN PARTY
At this "V for Victory" party, guests ate
food from the garden and dressed the
part of their favorite vegetable!

*A WAVE was a
woman sailor.*

*Play kits included everything
a real doctor or nurse used, from bandages
to candy medicine to cardboard scissors.*

THE VICTORY GAME
The object of this game was to draw and trade
blocks and chips until you could make the
Morse code symbol for *V*. Morse code
used dots and dashes for letters.
Three dots and a dash meant
"V for Victory."

CAPTAIN MIDNIGHT
Comic-book character Captain Midnight
was always on the lookout for enemy spies.
Readers could help—they just needed
a Captain Midnight Photo-Matic
Code-O-Graph Badge.

17

Play Ball!

Americans were learning to do without, but no one ever imagined doing without baseball! Most professional baseball players had given up their careers to go to war. But in May 1943, women stepped onto the field. Hundreds of female players tried out for the All-American Girls Professional Baseball League. Soon they were playing baseball for packed stands.

TRAINING

The new players spent days in training and nights in action. The league scheduled games six nights a week, with a double-header on the weekend.

Required beauty kits included cleansing cream, lipstick, rouge, deodorant, face powder, lotion, and hair products.

CHARM SCHOOL

Team owners wanted the women to "play like men" but still be feminine. As part of their training, the women attended "charm school." Instructors gave lessons in how to sit, walk, speak, and dress like a lady!

PEACHES AND BELLES

The first four professional teams were the Racine Belles, the Rockford Peaches, the Kenosha Comets, and the South Bend Blue Sox. More teams soon joined the league.

6 UNIFORM

During the war, mothers rose early and dressed for work in factories, offices, or Red Cross centers.

7 RADIO

The radio was the center of news and entertainment for 1940s families. There was no television.

8 BLACKOUT CURTAINS

In case of an *air-raid*, or enemy attack from the sky, families were prepared to "black out" their windows with heavy cloth so no light could be seen by an enemy plane.

9 TELEPHONE

The telephone company asked families not to use phones in the evening. They wanted phone lines left open so men and women in the military could make calls.

10 MENDING

Rather than buying new clothes, everyone learned to mend or change what they already had to make it last.

11 AIR-RAID SUPPLIES

Families kept air-raid supplies in the basement, including blankets, candles and matches, jugs of water, cans of food, a shovel, and sometimes even a cot.

12 MODEL AIRCRAFT

Boys and girls built 500,000 model airplanes that were used to train "spotters" to recognize the differences between American and enemy planes.

Victory Style

Making do meant making way for new fashions, too. The government needed 64 million shirts, 164 million coats, and 229 million pairs of pants for soldiers' uniforms. Cotton and wool material could not be wasted on civilian clothes, so there were no more frilly ruffles or poufy skirts. Instead, Americans invented all-new styles of clothing to help the nation win the war.

JOIN THE ARMY
Children wanted to dress in uniforms just as their fathers did overseas.

PATRIOTIC BEADS AND BANGLES
Girls wore rhinestone pins in the shape of a *V* for victory. And the president's Scottie dog, Fala, inspired all kinds of jewelry!

*Round collars, called **Peter Pan collars**, were popular for girls. They were styled after a costume worn by actress Maude Adams in the play **Peter Pan**.*

SEPARATES
Girls wore *separates*, or blouses and sweaters they could mix with different skirts or jumpers. Girls could make many outfits out of just a few clothes.

A law was passed limiting the amount of fabric that could be used in sleeves and hems.

BOBBY SOCKS
Girls wore bobby socks, which used much less material than tights. The term *bobby socks* came from the word *bob*, which means to shorten.

The straps on jumpers were extra long so they could be adjusted as a girl grew.

UNIFORM CHANGE
Before the war, Girl Scout uniforms had long zippers down the front. Since metal was needed for the war effort, the uniform was redesigned with buttons.

SADDLE SHOES
Saddle shoes were first popular in the 1920s as golf shoes. By the '40s, girls and boys wore them for both work and play.

DICKEYS

Removable collars called *dickeys* were worn instead of blouses under sweaters to save material.

Rickrack was a popular trim during World War Two, especially in "Flag Red" and "Victory Blue."

SHORT SKIRTS

Hems were let down as many times as possible. Then skirt lengths simply got shorter!

SEW, SAVE, AND SERVE FOR VICTORY

Women remade old clothes into new styles. There were patterns for turning a tablecloth into a new dress.

SHOCKING!

The most shocking new style of all was the two-piece bathing suit, which used less fabric than the more modest one-piece suit popular before the war.

This girl is tanning uniform stripes right onto her arm!

WOMEN IN PANTS

Women first wore pants to work in factories. But soon they became acceptable, and even glamorous, everyday wear.

FALLING UNDERWEAR

To save on rubber, underpants were sometimes made with ties rather than elastic waists. If the ties came loose, the underpants fell down!

FAKING IT

Silk and nylon were used to make parachutes, so during the war, there was none to spare for ladies' stockings. Women used leg makeup instead!

15

Playtime in Wartime

As the war went on, factories stopped making most toys. They needed to make war supplies instead. Then children started donating their own toys to the war effort. Anything made of metal or rubber could be melted down and made into life rafts, jeep tires, airplane parts, and gas masks. New toys were made of cardboard or wood and showed what was happening in the fight for victory.

WARTIME SACRIFICES
This girl gave up her old toys in a *scrap drive*. In scrap drives, children collected old pots, pans, foil, and cans and gave them to a collection center to be made into war equipment.

WATCH JOE GO!
This soldier jumped out of his jeep and into action when wound up. But a girl like Molly would have given him up. He's made of metal.

BANKS
Instead of piggy banks, children used banks shaped like tanks, ships, or the world. Each came with directions to use any saved money to buy war stamps and bonds.

World banks showed where troops were fighting.

PAPER DOLLS
Paper dolls no longer dressed in glamorous evening gowns. They wore the uniforms of Red Cross workers, army nurses, marines, and more.

MIDGIES
These miniature wooden toys came in an "army camp scene" set for just 98 cents. None of them was more than three inches long or tall.

Even pencil sharpeners went to war!

FIGHTERS FOR FREEDOM
War adventure series had girls and boys dreaming of the day they would be old enough to join the army or navy.

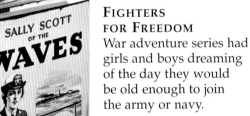

LITTLE ORPHAN ANNIE
Girls had their own comic-book heroes. Fifteen thousand children joined the Little Orphan Annie Junior Commandos. Annie encouraged members to win the war by gathering scrap.

VICTORY GARDEN PARTY
At this "V for Victory" party, guests ate food from the garden and dressed the part of their favorite vegetable!

A WAVE was a woman sailor.

Play kits included everything a real doctor or nurse used, from bandages to candy medicine to cardboard scissors.

THE VICTORY GAME
The object of this game was to draw and trade blocks and chips until you could make the Morse code symbol for *V*. Morse code used dots and dashes for letters. Three dots and a dash meant "V for Victory."

CAPTAIN MIDNIGHT
Comic-book character Captain Midnight was always on the lookout for enemy spies. Readers could help—they just needed a Captain Midnight Photo-Matic Code-O-Graph Badge.

17

Play Ball!

Americans were learning to do without, but no one ever imagined doing without baseball! Most professional baseball players had given up their careers to go to war. But in May 1943, women stepped onto the field. Hundreds of female players tried out for the All-American Girls Professional Baseball League. Soon they were playing baseball for packed stands.

TRAINING
The new players spent days in training and nights in action. The league scheduled games six nights a week, with a double-header on the weekend.

Required beauty kits included cleansing cream, lipstick, rouge, deodorant, face powder, lotion, and hair products.

CHARM SCHOOL
Team owners wanted the women to "play like men" but still be feminine. As part of their training, the women attended "charm school." Instructors gave lessons in how to sit, walk, speak, and dress like a lady!

PEACHES AND BELLES
The first four professional teams were the Racine Belles, the Rockford Peaches, the Kenosha Comets, and the South Bend Blue Sox. More teams soon joined the league.

JUNIOR TEAMS

For girls who dreamed of playing in the league, the first step was joining a junior team. Juniors had to be at least 12 years old and ready to play every Tuesday and Saturday.

BLOOMERS AND STRAWBERRIES

To make sure players appeared ladylike, uniforms had skirts and short bloomers. Without pants, sliding into base meant getting painful scrapes. The women called them "strawberries."

Milwaukee Chicks catcher Dorothy Maguire at bat

TOUGH PLAY

The ladies didn't play like men—some people thought they played better. There were more stolen bases in their games than in most men's major-league games.

THE END OF THE GAME

When the war ended and major-league baseball returned, the All-American Girls League struggled. By 1954, it had become a thing of the past.

OFFICIAL PROGRAM

ALL-AMERICAN GIRLS PROFESSIONAL BALL LEAGUE

BUY WAR BONDS

Hometown, USA

From women on baseball fields to bicycles on the roads, the war certainly changed life on the home front. But it was hard to get discouraged. There was too much to do! People rallied together to keep their communities running—and prepared for war.

① WAR PLANT
Companies built and refitted factories as fast as they could to help manufacture all the new ships, planes, and guns America needed.

② RUBBER DRIVES
The government needed rubber so badly it accepted car tires, garden hoses, buckets of galoshes, even rain slickers.

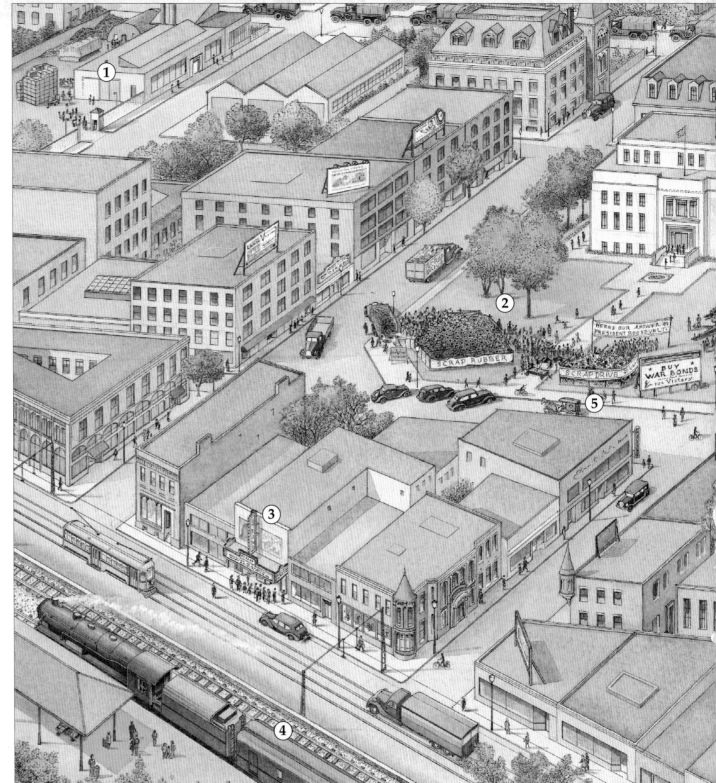

③ THEATER
Theaters stayed open 24 hours a day so that factory workers on both day and night shifts could see movies.

④ TRAINS
Trains steamed through stations around the clock, carrying troops, tanks, and other weapons to ports on both the East and West Coasts.

⑩ JAPANESE AMERICANS
Japanese Americans were forced to leave their homes and sell their businesses after the bombing of Pearl Harbor. They were kept in special camps away from the public. People feared they might side with the enemy.

⑨ USO CANTEEN
At special clubs called *canteens*, volunteers offered food, fun, and entertainment.

⑧ TRAVEL TRICKS
Families traveled around the old-fashioned way—by walking, biking, or taking the bus.

⑦ GROCERY
Stores advertised when they had hard-to-find foods, and women lined up to get what they could.

⑤ OLD-FASHIONED HORSEPOWER
Gasoline was hard to get. It wasn't unusual to see a horse and wagon on the road!

⑥ CIVIL DEFENSE CORPS
Volunteers joined the Civil Defense Corps. Many worked as plane spotters. The "CD" logo, a white triangle with red letters on a blue circle, could be seen all over communities.

The Enemy *in the* Sky

Molly, Linda, and Susan loved to play in the pretend bomb shelter they had made under the card table in Molly's basement. Most air raids in America were just practice drills. Families hurried and huddled together under blankets in the basement until the all-clear siren sounded. But for children, air-raid drills were exciting, and even fun.

THE REAL THING
In other countries, like England, where the bombing was real, air raids were not a game. Every night, Emily said, she had to sit in the dark, waiting, hearing explosions. When she came out, a house she'd walked by every day might be gone.

PATROLS
Air-raid wardens walked the streets during a drill. They made sure that every house had drawn its blackout curtains and that all lights were out.

STICKERS
Glow-in-the-dark stickers helped families stay safe and have fun during blackout drills.

PITCH-BLACK
Even car headlights had to be covered during a blackout. Flaps that looked like eyelashes made sure any light shined down, and hopefully wouldn't be seen from the sky.

Hundreds of uses for
BLACKOUT ★ KUTOUTS
THE NEW WONDER MATERIAL
Glows in the dark

FOR FUN
FOR UTILITY
JONES SHOES
2141

BLACKOUT
THE BOMBING PLANES HAVE BEEN SIGHTED. THEY WILL ARRIVE IN EXACTLY TWO MINUTES. CAN YOU BLACKOUT ALL THE LIGHTS IN TIME TO SAVE THE TOWN

GAMES
Even games were reminders that lights had to be blocked during an air-raid drill.

BI-5

The Tube

Night and day the Germans bombed London. Anyone caught on the street when the air-raid siren went off dashed for the *tube*, or subway. People spent entire nights there, huddled together for safety and comfort.

Leaving Home

Many British parents, like Emily's, sent their children out of London in order to protect them. The children wore tags that told their destinations. Adults made sure they boarded the right trains and ships.

Truth in Superstition?

For 900 years, ravens had nested by the Tower of London. People said they protected the city. During World War Two, only a single raven remained.

Tears and Courage

Claire Bloom was ten years old when the Germans began bombing her country. Like Emily Bennett, Claire left England to come to America. The day her father took her to the docks was drizzly and cold. When she saw the ship, Claire suddenly understood what was happening. She was leaving home.

Claire was lucky. She was traveling to America with her brother and her mother. As they settled into their cabin, Claire's father began to weep bitterly. Claire had never seen a grown man cry. She began to sob, too. She was certain she would never see her father again.

On the voyage across the Atlantic Ocean, Claire had to be brave. The ship zigzagged to avoid torpedo attacks by German submarines. Claire and her mother and brother slept in their clothes, ready to abandon ship at a minute's notice. It took ten days for Claire and her mother and brother to arrive in America safely.

One day, Claire would return to England and see her father again. For now, though, a new home and a strange new land lay ahead— America.

SAFE[V]

UNITED STATES COMMITTEE FOR THE
CARE OF EUROPEAN CHILDREN, INC.
MEMBER AGENCY of the NATIONAL WAR FUND, Inc.

THE TUBE
Night and day the Germans bombed London. Anyone caught on the street when the air-raid siren went off dashed for the *tube*, or subway. People spent entire nights there, huddled together for safety and comfort.

LEAVING HOME
Many British parents, like Emily's, sent their children out of London in order to protect them. The children wore tags that told their destinations. Adults made sure they boarded the right trains and ships.

TRUTH IN SUPERSTITION?
For 900 years, ravens had nested by the Tower of London. People said they protected the city. During World War Two, only a single raven remained.

Tears and Courage

Claire Bloom was ten years old when the Germans began bombing her country. Like Emily Bennett, Claire left England to come to America. The day her father took her to the docks was drizzly and cold. When she saw the ship, Claire suddenly understood what was happening. She was leaving home.

Claire was lucky. She was traveling to America with her brother and her mother. As they settled into their cabin, Claire's father began to weep bitterly. Claire had never seen a grown man cry. She began to sob, too. She was certain she would never see her father again.

On the voyage across the Atlantic Ocean, Claire had to be brave. The ship zigzagged to avoid torpedo attacks by German submarines. Claire and her mother and brother slept in their clothes, ready to abandon ship at a minute's notice. It took ten days for Claire and her mother and brother to arrive in America safely.

One day, Claire would return to England and see her father again. For now, though, a new home and a strange new land lay ahead— America.

SAFE

UNITED STATES COMMITTEE FOR THE CARE OF EUROPEAN CHILDREN, INC.
MEMBER AGENCY of the NATIONAL WAR FUND, Inc.

Margaret's Story

Americans learned about the bombing of London from newspaper reports. The attack was called "the Blitz." It was short for *blitzkrieg* (BLITS-kreeg), a German word for "lightning war." Bill White was one of many American newspaper reporters who went to London in 1940 to write about the Blitz. He and his wife had no children. They knew that the parents of many British children had died in the air raids. Bill hoped that while he was in London he could adopt a child to take home with him to America.

He went to an orphanage, a home for children whose parents had died. The *matron*, the woman who cared for the children, brought him a little boy named John. John stood before Bill, holding his cap in his hands and staring at his feet. Then the door opened again. The *matron* pushed forward another orphan, a girl. She was tiny, just four years old. She wore a hooded red coat and shabby red leggings. She rubbed her dry eyes, over and over again, one first and then the other with her tiny fists.

"I don't know what to make of little Margaret," said the matron. "She is naughty. She won't play with the other children, and she doesn't eat."

Bill took the two children to a boarding school. Heidi, the teacher, promised to care for the children until the time came for Bill to return to America. Little John went to Heidi at once, but Margaret held back, rubbing her eyes hard.

During the day, Bill worked. At night, he visited the children. Margaret made progress. She now drank her milk and ate her dinner. She showed Bill one of her finger paintings. The paper was a swirl of colorful shapes. "It's a little girl and her mum," Margaret told Bill. "But her mum went away and never came back."

Slowly, Heidi and Bill pieced together the puzzle of Margaret's past. During the Blitz, a German bomb had killed her mother and father and blown up their home. Margaret didn't really understand what that meant. At the orphanage, she had kept asking to go home. But each time she asked, she was spanked. "You must never cry for what you have lost," the matron had scolded her. "You must push the tears back into your eyes."

That was why Margaret rubbed her eyes.

At last the day came for Bill to go home. He was allowed only one seat on the airplane. He could take only one orphan on his lap—in place of his luggage. Bill had to choose. Reluctantly, he took John back to the orphanage. Then he returned to the boarding school for Margaret. But this time when Bill reached for her, Margaret slapped his hands away.

"She thinks you are abandoning her," Heidi explained sadly.

On the train from London to the airport, Margaret refused to speak or even sit close to Bill. She rubbed and rubbed her eyes. At a train stop, Bill stepped outside for a moment to see where they were. Margaret suddenly started to scream. "Don't go!" she cried. Bill turned and she ran into his arms. Fear pinched her face. "Daddy won't leave you," Bill told her softly, "not ever."

And then, finally, Margaret began to cry.

Tough Times, Brave Smiles

Families all across America watched sons, brothers, and husbands ship out to war. Left behind to face life on their own, the women and children were sometimes frightened and lonely. But they were also proud of America's part in the war. They believed winning the war would make the world a better place for everyone, so they did whatever it took to support the war on the home front.

PITCHING IN
Everyone worried about their relatives away at war. But worry wouldn't bring them home. Instead, people all across America worked together, just like in Molly's Lend-a-Hand school project.

From the book Molly Learns a Lesson

Junior Red Cross members packed boxes of toys and games for children overseas.

WINDOW BANNERS
To show their pride and love, people hung blue stars in their windows, one for each family member who was at war. If someone was killed, the family hung a gold star.

WHAT CAN I DO?
Children saved metal, paper, and rubber. They rolled bandages and knit sweaters, socks, and blankets.

Schools sponsored scrap drives, held plane-identification classes, and sold war stamps.

We Are Ready ★ What About You?
Join the
SCHOOLS AT WAR
Program

Railroads hired women as "trainmen," who opened the doors and operated the brakes.

WORKING WOMEN

As men went away to fight, many women volunteered for organizations like the Red Cross. Others did whatever was needed. They pumped gas, became firefighters, even worked as lumberjacks.

JOBS FOR ALL?

Job opportunities weren't open to everyone. Black workers had trouble finding jobs. When they did, they were paid less than white workers.

Women like this dairy farmer kept farms running so Americans had enough food.

VICTORY WAITS ON YOUR FINGERS

KEEP 'EM FLYING, MISS U.S.A.

UNCLE SAM NEEDS STENOGRAPHERS! • GET CIVIL SERVICE INFORMATION AT YOUR LOCAL POST OFFICE
U.S. CIVIL SERVICE COMMISSION, WASHINGTON, D.C.

Women secretaries filled many government office jobs. They called themselves "GGs," or "Government Girls."

We Can Do It!

Many women moved to new towns to find jobs at war plants or shipyards. They made the ships, planes, and weapons soldiers needed. Some factory owners thought women were not strong enough to weld metal seams on a warship or fire *rivets*, or bolts, into airplane panels all day. They thought women should stay home and raise children. The women proved them wrong. They managed factory work—and factory life—as well as any man.

TODAY'S SCHEDULE

7am - leave factory
8am - send children to school
8:30 am - grocery shop
10:00 am - go to bed
11:30 am - lunch for children
12:30 pm - back to bed
3:00 pm - children home from school
3 - 7pm - laundry, clean, cook dinner
7:00 pm - back to bed
10:00 pm - leave for work

NO VACANCY!
So many women moved into factory towns that housing became a huge problem. Companies set up temporary trailer camps to help, but even they were quickly filled to overflowing.

ON THE JOB
Women faced grueling days— or nights. This *swing shift*, or night shift, schedule was common.

ON THEIR OWN
Children learned to take care of themselves and accepted new responsibilities in order to make it possible for their mothers to work.

Crossing guards, now at work or war, were replaced with papier-mâché statues to warn drivers.

MICHIGAN US 16

SCHOOL ZONE SLOW

Finding housing was especially difficult for mothers. In tiny rooms, dresser drawers doubled as cribs!

ENDLESS PRODUCTION
Nine-hour workdays and a six-day workweek were the factory standard. Assembly lines never stopped.

These assembly line workers are polishing the noses of A-20 bomber planes.

ROSIE THE RIVETER
Newspaper writers gave the new factory workers a name based on a popular song, "Rosie the Riveter." The refrain was: "She's making history working for victory!"

WE'RE BUYING AT LEAST 10%

THIS IS **MY** FIGHT TOO!

WAGES
Women weren't just working for victory. Most had to go to work in order to support their families. A serviceman's salary simply wasn't enough to live on.

Independence

Despite the hardships, women enjoyed their work. They gained confidence as they learned new skills. They earned better wages than ever before and were able to support themselves, often for the first time. They were independent and enjoyed freedoms women didn't have before the war. They proved that a woman's place was definitely not just at home. One woman wrote to her husband overseas:

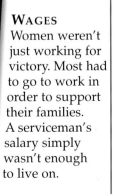

"I must admit I'm not exactly the same girl you left. I'm twice as independent as I used be. Sometimes I think I've become hard as nails. I've been living exactly as I want to."

Women in Uniform

While thousands of women went to work in factories, thousands more joined the military. In 1942, the United States Congress established the first military unit just for women, called the Women's Army Corps, or WAC. Some congressmen were against women in uniform, predicting the "ladies" would break down in tears during tough times. But the new recruits took military training in stride.

CLOTHING WAREHOUSE.

GETTING IN GEAR
The first stop after joining the army was a clothing warehouse. Clothes, even underwear, came in one color—olive drab!

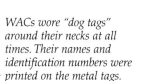

WACs wore "dog tags" around their necks at all times. Their names and identification numbers were printed on the metal tags.

MILITARY HOURS
A bugle call at 6:00 A.M. meant *Reveille*, wake-up time for WACs. They were expected to be up until taps was played at 10:00 at night.

① *The army issued hats for exercise, summer, and drill.*

② *Each WAC got two pairs of gloves—one for work, one for dress.*

③ *A small packet of mending supplies, called a **housewife**, included needle and thread.*

ON DETAIL
Daily schedules included *details*, or work assignments. The most dreaded was KP, or kitchen patrol. Recruits had to help the cooks and then clean up after a meal. *Latrine*, or bathroom, duty wasn't much better.

TRAINING
Field training included running through obstacle courses, bellying under barbed wire, and climbing 30-foot cargo nets.

Although women soldiers could not fight in combat, many still went through combat training.

③

④

U.S. ARMY
Writing Tablet

②

WAAC

⑤

⑤ *The lower level of a foot-locker held a WAC's clothes: underwear, four pairs of shoes, a bathrobe, pajamas, five shirts, a jacket, and an exercise suit.*

CHOICES
Women trained to work as mechanics, air-traffic controllers, electricians, mapmakers, photographers, metal-smiths, plumbers, engineers, and more. There was something for everyone in the army.

④ *Soldiers wrote letters on "V-mail." V-mail forms were photographed. The film was sent in place of the letter. Film took up less room than regular mail.*

CLOSE INSPECTION
WACs had to be ready at any time for an inspection. Footlockers had to be packed neatly, and beds had to be made with exactly six inches between the pillow and the top of the sheet.

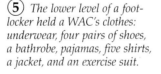

Topographic Draftsman
ARMY GROUND FORCES

WOMAN'S PLACE IN WAR
The Army of the United States has 239 kinds of jobs for women
WOMEN'S ARMY CORPS

ind in Their Veins

Emig
Eger   Disston

Eger   Disston

The Women's Airforce Service Pilots, or WASPs, gave almost 2,000 women a chance to serve their country while doing what they loved best—flying. The women tested new aircraft, delivered planes cross-country, trained male pilots, and more. "As long as planes fly overhead, the skies of America are free, and that's what all of us are fighting for," said one WASP. "That we are being allowed to help keep that sky free is the most beautiful thing I have ever known!"

AVIATION ENTERPRISES LTD.

Avenger Field, in dusty Sweetwater, Texas, was the only military flying school for women in the United States.

THE WISHING WELL

A WASP had to prove her skill by flying *check rides* with an instructor. For luck, each girl would throw a coin in Avenger Field's well before her ride. If she passed, her fellow WASPs threw *her* in the well to get her coin back!

BORN TO FLY

Many recruits had struggled to learn to fly, taking odd jobs to pay for lessons and driving hours to air fields. When they finally got their wings, "It was wonderful— and they paid us!" said one WASP.

GROUND SCHOOL

WASPs spent 400 hours in ground school studying physics, navigation, weather code, and more. Here, trainees are learning what high-altitude flight will feel like.

WASP Mascot
No one flew without the WASPs' official logo on her jacket. Fifinella was a fairy character that WASPs said watched over them.

Aim and Shoot
WASP pilots did not fly in combat missions. They did, however, tow targets for male gunners to shoot at for practice.

Clipboards with maps and flight plans were worn strapped around the pilot's leg.

Ready for Takeoff!
To take off in this B-25 bomber, WASPs had to go through six checklists with 76 steps. There were another five checklists for landing.

① *The plane's speed showed here. The B-25 could go up to 300 miles per hour.*

② *Pilots could fly using only the instrument panel. This "artificial horizon" helped them keep their bearings.*

③ *Engine trouble would show up on these gauges, one for each side of the plane.*

④ *Fuel gauge*

⑤ *Pulling back on the throttles increased the plane's speed.*

⑥ *Both pilot and copilot could control the plane using the control yokes, much like steering wheels on cars.*

Winning Their Wings
More than 1,000 women "won their wings" at Avenger Field. "The belief that army flying is for men has gone into the ash can," *Life* magazine reported.

Dogs for Defense!

Fighting men and women were the backbone of the military. But another type of soldier—one with four legs—saved many lives and may have helped to shorten the war. The military recruited and trained hundreds of K-9 soldiers to be messengers, rescuers, scouts, and pack animals. They served on the home front patrolling coastline beaches and protecting military installments as well as overseas in the roar of battle.

PROUD TO SERVE
People volunteered their dogs for service. A dog had to weigh at least 50 pounds, be at least 20 inches tall, and be between the ages of one and five.

MEALTIME
New recruits, used to treats from their owners' tables, turned up their noses at dinner. But after a few days of hard training, the new GI food looked absolutely delicious.

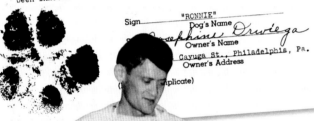

BASIC TRAINING
Handlers taught dogs basic commands: heel, sit, down, come, and stay. Then the dogs learned their first war skill—how to crawl low to the ground.

SENTRY WORK

A dog's sense of smell and hearing are better than a human's. *Sentry*, or guard, dogs saved countless lives by detecting intruders. One soldier said his dog was better than seven men.

ADVANCED TRAINING

Dogs learned to climb ramps, jump obstacles, and crawl through barbed wire. Some even learned to parachute. The hardest lesson was learning not to fear gunfire.

HONORABLE DISCHARGE

At the end of the war, dogs were trained to go back to civilian life. By 1947, every volunteer dog had been returned to its owner.

IN THE LINE OF DUTY

Dogs were often wounded. Caesar was shot twice while saving his handler. An enemy soldier had crawled close to their hiding place. He was about to toss a grenade when Caesar attacked. The enemy dropped his weapon.

War Dog

The Doberman was determined. He could see his destination, and no enemy fire would stop him. Attached to the collar around his neck was a waterproof metal capsule. It had to be delivered. His handler was part of a troop cut off from their command post. Only the messages the dog carried could reach them.

The ground exploded with a flash of fire and thunder. Clods of dirt shot into the air. But the Doberman raced on, leaping over a fallen tree. Another grenade blast rocked the ground. Ahead was a stream. The dog was a streak of motion, swimming across and scrabbling up the steep bank. Without a pause, he bellied under a barbed-wire fence and raced forward. Finally he reached his goal. His handler grabbed the capsule and opened it. Inside was a map and an important message about the enemy's movements. The wild dash under enemy fire would be repeated again and again until, exhausted, the dog had to rest. Bravery, courage, and daring. It was all in a day's work for a war dog.

Time Out

Homesick soldiers and home front workers all needed an escape from the pressures of war. And they found it! Many people flocked to live theater shows. In big cities, some dance halls played big-band dance music to crowds every night of the week. A little bit of fun kept everyone's spirits up.

From the book Changes for Molly

HURRAY FOR THE U.S.A.
Small towns like Molly's put on variety shows to support the war effort. They might benefit a veterans' hospital or raise money for the Red Cross.

ON THE ROAD
The United Service Organization, or USO, tried to make sure troops overseas had fun, too. They organized tours for Hollywood stars, like Bob Hope, often near the front lines.

USO
UNITED SERVICE ORGANIZATIONS

CANTEENS

All across America, canteens created "homes away from home" for servicemen. A lonely soldier could always count on a sandwich, a cup of coffee, and a friendly smile at a canteen.

The Stage Door Canteen was so popular a movie was made about it in 1943.

THE "IN" PLACE

The Stage Door Canteen was on Broadway in New York City, where many movie and radio stars lived. The stars often showed up to sing or dance with the soldiers.

OUCH!

Dance floors got so crowded that "we couldn't help getting kicked in the shins and ankles," said one woman. "I'm due for my war medal any day now!"

A SPECIAL RECORD

In some canteens, a soldier could record a message on a record and send it home.

A Special Welcome

When Rae Wilson learned that a military train was going to stop in her hometown of North Platte, Nebraska, she knew just what she wanted to do. Hundreds of local boys, including her brother, would be on board. The train would stop for only an hour, but that was enough time for a special welcome.

That afternoon a large crowd gathered at the train station. The people brought cakes, cookies, and gifts to give to their sons and brothers and sweethearts. They cheered as the train pulled in.

But Rae's brother wasn't on the train. The soldiers weren't even from Nebraska! The people were disappointed, but they gave their gifts to the soldiers anyway. Some mothers and wives cried, but they were happy just the same. They had brightened the day for boys on their way to war.

Walking home, Rae Wilson got an idea. Why not meet every military train? Rae opened her own canteen at the train station. About 1,000 soldiers a day stepped inside! The people of North Platte, Nebraska, were happy to entertain them.

Red Cross Spirit

Wherever the soldiers went, American Red Cross workers soon followed. They worked 14 hours a day, setting up "welcome centers" where soldiers at the front lines could take a break from the war. Workers cooked food, organized events, and were always ready to listen. Margaret Cotter volunteered to be a Red Cross worker when she was just a few years older than Molly's sister Jill. Her first assignment was halfway around the world—in northern Africa!

RED CROSS ARRIVALS
Margaret traveled to Africa with 60 other Red Cross girls. The trip took 50 days. When the coast finally came into view, she wasn't sure what to expect. But she knew one thing—she was entering a battle zone.

SIGHT-SEEING
The Red Cross sent Margaret to Cairo to wait for orders. The ancient Egyptian monuments fascinated her. "I felt we were midgets before monsters," Margaret said while gazing at the pyramids.

THE CLUBMOBILE
Margaret and her puppy always met pilots coming back from a mission at the runway. In her "Clubmobile" she kept games and magazines, hot coffee, and doughnuts.

Benghazi

When the troops advanced, so did the Red Cross workers. Margaret and her puppy traveled with the soldiers across the desert to the war-torn city of Benghazi on the Mediterranean Sea. Fighting had destroyed most of the city, and the people had fled.

Margaret took over one of the few buildings still standing. Inches of dirt lay on the floor. The ceilings were covered with cobwebs. The doors and windows had been blown out by bombs, and there was no electricity or furniture. She set to work. Margaret removed rubble and scrubbed away sand and filth. She discovered colorful tiles on the walls and floors. She made chairs out of the protective packing bombs were shipped in! Finally she hung out a big white flag with the Red Cross on it. The center was open. That night, tired but happy, Margaret at last thought of a special name for her puppy: Benghazi, or Benjy for short.

DESERT LIFE
At the air base, Margaret learned to use her steel helmet as a washbasin and to sleep on an army cot with no sheets or pillow.

GOOD COMPANY
Margaret soon received orders to set up a welcome center—at an air base in the middle of the desert. She would live in a tent. Margaret was thrilled. "I didn't want conditions to be any better for me than they were for the soldiers," she said. Still, to keep her company, Margaret adopted an unwanted dachshund puppy.

Movies

Modern Screen

On Saturday afternoons, Molly could almost forget all about the war. Saturday was movie day! One week, she might see an adventure movie about a boy and his courageous dog, Lassie. Another week, she might watch a scary movie about an Earth invasion from outer space. Fun fantasies helped everyone escape the troubles of war for a while. But the war did come to the big screen, too. Patriotic movies were designed to remind everyone of what they were fighting for.

From the book *The American Girls Club Handbook*

CAPITOL
TOM DRAKE
"COURAGE OF LASSIE"

THE PLACE TO BE
For ten cents, Molly could spend nearly all day in the theater. It was just like a party! Girls and boys cheered and booed and talked to friends during the show.

LASSIE
The first Lassie movie was shown in 1943. Lassie became so popular that books, comics, and later even a TV series were made about her.

FREE TOYS!
An afternoon at the movies included a cartoon and a short Western with cowboys and horses. Companies even gave away toys, like this doll of Dopey from Disney's *Snow White and the Seven Dwarfs*!

In real life, actor Ronald Reagan, above, would one day become president of the United States.

WAR FILMS
Movies made military service seem glamorous and exciting. Heroes always fought and won exciting battles against German and Japanese "bad guys."

FAYE CONSTANCE BENNETT NANCY KELLY
TAIL SPIN
A 20TH CENTURY-FOX PICTURE
DARRYL F. ZANUCK IN CHARGE OF PRODUCTION

Tail Spin was all about WASPs' courage in the line of duty.

HOME FRONT MOVIES
One of the most popular movies of 1944, *Since You Went Away*, showed the hardships of homefront family life. It was about a family like Molly's, with a father away at war.

Shirley Temple, Claudette Colbert, and Jennifer Jones receive a letter from the front in Since You Went Away.

NEWSREELS

LOWELL THOMAS Commentator
MOVIETONE NEWS
Produced by EDMUND REEK

Along with the cartoons and Westerns, moviegoers always saw a black and white newsreel that reported on the progress of the war. Newsreels brought "The Eyes and Ears of the World" to the screen, showing actual land, air, and sea battles. It was obvious, even to the youngest children, that the newsreels were not part of a movie, but were real life. When a newsreel came on, some people would begin to cry. Others shouted at the images of Hitler and the German and Japanese soldiers. And some were frightened. "I felt I was actually there," remembered one girl, "and I would be terrified for days afterward."

Hitler shows the Nazi salute.

Horror and Hope

News about the war was everywhere, on the radio, in the newspapers, and at the movies. But some stories were too shocking to believe. When reporters said that Adolf Hitler's Nazi troops were killing millions of people, including Jews, in prisons called *concentration camps*, many people thought it was just *propaganda*, or stories meant to make the enemy look evil. After all, in pictures taken from planes, the prisons looked like work camps. But something horrible really *was* happening. After the war's end, the killing came to be called the *Holocaust*.

THE PRISONERS
Prisoners traveled to camps in railroad cars. Upon arrival, Nazi guards separated the women and girls from the men and boys. Most would not see one another again.

PUT TO WORK
A sign over the entrance to one Nazi camp read "Work will make you free." In fact, people were worked to death. And anyone too weak or ill, or too young or old, to work was killed.

MILK CAN MESSAGE
In Poland, Jews wrote about what was happening to them at the camps. They put their papers inside three milk cans, which they buried. They desperately hoped that someone would discover the papers and learn the truth.

Two milk cans were found, but one remains buried.

TO FLY AWAY
A prisoner carved this butterfly toy and smuggled it into a children's barracks. It was a symbol of freedom and a message not to give up hope.

I feel like a songbird whose wings have been clipped and who is hurling himself against the bars of his cage. I can feel the suffering of millions and yet, if I look up into the heavens, I think that it will all come out right – that this cruelty will end and that peace will return.
– Anne Frank

HIDING

Anne Frank was 13 when her family went into hiding in an attic to avoid being sent to a camp. But in 1944, she and her family were discovered. A friend found Anne's diary. She saved it to give to Anne when she returned, but Anne never did. She died in a camp.

RESCUE BOAT

People from many countries, including Germany, risked their lives to save people from the camps. These people had no weapons, so they had to be clever. In Nazi-controlled Denmark, fishing boats like this one secretly ferried thousands of Jews to safety.

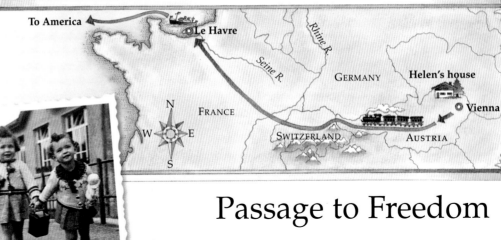

Passage to Freedom

Helen, right, with her rag doll

One night at bedtime in 1938, Helen Neuman's mother told her to "Sleep in your clothes and your shoes and socks. And take your little rag doll with you. Don't let her out of your sight." Helen didn't understand, but she did as she was told. That night, she and her parents left everyone they loved and eveything they owned. They took only one small suitcase and Helen's rag doll.

Helen was a Jewish girl who lived in Vienna, Austria. By 1938, Nazi soldiers were rounding up Jews in her country. Helen's father had even been arrested. He had bribed a guard into letting him go, but he knew that escape was the only way to survive.

Helen's father sewed all of the family's money into the lining of his jacket and, unknown to Helen, into her doll.

That money got the family to the Austrian border by train. Then they crossed on foot the mountains called the Alps, trying to reach Switzerland. There they were turned back because of their passports. They were marked with a big red J for *Juden*, or Jew. The Nazis weren't letting Jews leave the country. A kind border guard looked the other way and let the family find shelter, but only temporarily. They soon had to move on to Le Havre, France, where a ship would take them to America.

Helen would never return to Austria to see her aunts and uncles and grandparents again. But she was very lucky. Her rag doll was opened and sewn up so many times that she fell apart. The doll never made it to America, but with her help, Helen and her family did.

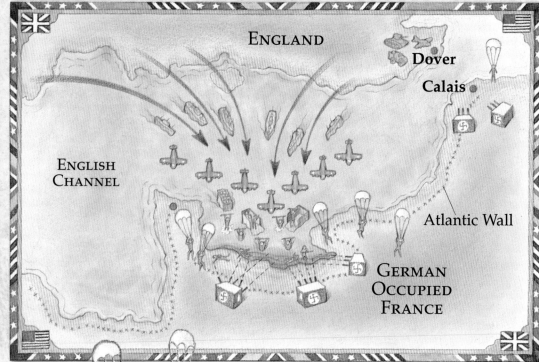

ENGLAND

Dover

Calais

ENGLISH CHANNEL

Atlantic Wall

GERMAN OCCUPIED FRANCE

D-Day

D-Day, the day of the invasion, began before dawn on June 6. Hundreds of paratroopers and pilots took to the sky, and thousands of ships pushed into the channel and headed for France.

Troops plunged into the water and waded toward the beaches. Most of the first men to reach land were killed.

Invasion

During the spring of 1944, while Anne Frank was still hiding in an attic, more than 400,000 American soldiers shipped overseas to England. No one knew their final destination, but everyone suspected something *big* was about to happen. And something was. Across the English Channel was Nazi-controlled France. To win the war, American and British generals planned a massive invasion of France. If they could attack and overwhelm the Nazis along the French coast, they could begin marching toward Germany. This one invasion would make or break the war.

THE ATLANTIC WALL
The Germans knew that an invasion was coming, but they didn't know where. So they built a "wall" of explosive mines and spider-like tetrahedra (teh-tra-HEE-dra), which would rip the bottoms out of boats when the tide came in.

Success!

By nightfall, the Allied troops had taken the beaches of Normandy, France. It was just the beginning. Now the Allies needed to land thousands of trucks, tanks, and other supplies. They needed a force strong enough to march right through France and into Germany.

The survivors of D-Day were exhausted and shocked. Their success had a terrible price. More than 9,000 men had died.

From the book Molly Saves the Day

Driving on Water

The supply ships docked at floating harbors. From the harbors, engineers built floating roads to shore. The idea was simple—just like the path to shore that Molly built during Camp Gowonagin's Color War.

Liberation

The Allies moved across France, freeing Paris in August. By December, troops were at the German border, ready for the final push to end the war in Europe.

Allied soldiers often had candy to share with French children.

TOP SECRET

The Germans thought the D-Day attack would come at Calais, just a short distance across the channel from Dover, England. The Allies worked hard to make it seem as if they were right. Preparations for D-Day involved a lot of secrets!

The D-Day attack was code-named Operation Overlord, and more secret codes were used to plan every part of it. When several of the code words turned up in the *London Daily Telegraph*'s crossword puzzle, officials panicked. But it turned out to be just a coincidence.

Fake inflatable balloon tanks and trucks were "parked" all around Dover so that German spy planes would see what looked like troops gathering.

Even on D-Day itself, the Germans were confused. Hundreds of dummy paratroopers were dropped behind German lines at Calais. Planes also dropped foil sheets over the coast. They looked like bombs on German radar.

Caring for Casualties

D-Day had been a success, but as in every battle, many men lost their lives, and many more were seriously wounded. The soldiers counted on the Army Nurse Corps to care for the casualties. The nurses were trained to work in combat zones, and they followed the front lines. But no amount of training could prepare them to care for as many as 200 men at once. Many nurses worked 24-hour shifts to keep up with demand.

Nurses Are Needed Now!

FOR SERVICE IN THE
ARMY NURSE CORPS

IF YOU ARE A REGISTERED NURSE AND NOT YET 45 YEARS OF AGE
APPLY TO THE SURGEON GENERAL, UNITED STATES ARMY,
WASHINGTON 25, D. C., OR TO ANY RED CROSS PROCUREMENT OFFICE

NURSES
Nurses who joined the army had four weeks of training to prepare for battlefields. They hiked 20 miles a day carrying 30-pound packs and crawled through trenches and barbed-wire obstacle courses.

ON THE MOVE
Some nurses followed the troops onto the battlefield, providing the quickest medical help possible. They pulled up their tents and moved on nearly every day.

TRAVELING HOSPITALS
Nurses worked on ships, trains, and planes, taking the wounded from battle fronts to safer ground. There were more than 400 beds below deck on a hospital ship. Doctors operated 24 hours a day.

MEDICAL SUPPLIES
Supplies were always running short. Nurses made bandages by tearing up clothing, donated their own blood, and used pants as stretchers.

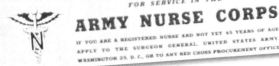

IN THE FACE OF DANGER

Army nurses faced more danger than any other women serving in the military. More than 200 were killed on duty. Many more were taken prisoner.

Smiling with relief, these army nurses are being released from a prisoner-of-war camp after almost three years.

Prisoners were given meal cards, but there was rarely enough food. The camps were too crowded.

MANILA INTERNMENT CAMP
NOVEMBER 1944 MEAL TICKET NO: 1493
NAME: *Gates, Marcia*
ROOM NO: 39
SIGNATURE: *M. Newsom*

The Red Cross symbol identified doctors and nurses and helped protect them from being fired upon.

LARGE
BATTLE DRESSING
STERILIZED—CAMOUFLAGED
U. S. ARMY
CARLISLE MODEL
(TO OPEN FULL TAB)

STOCK NO. 2-115
3 inches   5 yards
BANDAGE
PLASTER OF PARIS

SIX IODINE SWABS
EACH TUBE CONTAINS
1½ CC of 2% Tincture of Iodine
(45% Alcohol)
. . . . POISON . . . .
Mfg. By McCleery Glass Products
Willowbrook, California

Iodine cleans minor wounds.

Sulfanilamide tablets fight infection.

Tourniquets help stop bleeding.

Dogs were specially trained to find wounded men on battlefields. They tried to keep the men awake until nurses could reach them.

DEATH OF A SOLDIER

June Wandrey earned seven World War Two battle stars for her work as a combat nurse. As her letter shows, doctors and nurses could not save every soldier.

*Dearest Family,
…Many wounded soldiers' faces still haunt my memory. I recall one eighteen-year-old who had just been brought in from the ambulance. He looked up at me trustingly and asked, "How am I doing, nurse?" I put my hands around his face, kissed his forehead, and said, "You are doing just fine, soldier." He smiled sweetly. And then he died.
Very tired, June*

A Christmas Surprise

Martha Gellhorn was a newspaper reporter. As a war correspondent she had crossed the English Channel in the hours after the D-Day invasion. She traveled with American troops and wrote stories about what she saw. In late December 1944, an army sergeant was driving Martha in a jeep along a country road in Germany. All around her, the scenery looked just like a Christmas card. "At sunrise and sunset the snow was pink and the forests grew smoky and soft," she wrote. From a distance the country villages seemed to snuggle in the snow. Up close, however, Martha saw they were mostly burned buildings and rubble. Overhead, American attack planes flew in formation.

"The war front was just up the road, and the danger was far from past," Martha said. But even in wartime, people found happiness in the world around them. "We decided, like millions of other people, that we were sick of war; what we really wanted to do was borrow a sled and go coasting."

And so, at the top of a steep hill, the driver pulled the jeep to the side of the road. As he and Martha climbed out, they heard children laughing and shouting. There on the other side of the hill were dozens of children. They slid and bounced on sleds in the snow. Gunfire still rumbled in the distance, but the children didn't seem to hear it. Or if they heard it, they didn't care. The war didn't seem very real to Martha now either as she stood in the snow and watched the children. Their happiness was a perfect Christmas surprise. They reminded her that peace would come again.

That Christmas, people all around the world began to dream. Perhaps this would be the last year of war. Perhaps next year all the soldiers and nurses, all the Red Cross workers and war correspondents would be home with their children, celebrating the holidays.

"Children are plenty smart," the driver of the jeep said after a few minutes. "What I mean is, children have the right idea. What people ought to do is put down their guns and go sleigh riding."

And that's just what he and Martha did.

V-E Day

The dream of peace came true on May 7, 1945. A delegation of German officers arrived at a British army camp near Hamburg, Germany. They had come to surrender. They sat stiffly while the commanding officer of the Allied forces read the terms of surrender, and then they signed the surrender document. News correspondents rushed away to write about the good news. The war in Europe was over at last!

DANCING FOR JOY
"Joy was on everyone's face," remembered one homefront girl. Strangers were even dancing together in the middle of the road!

ENGLAND HEARS THE NEWS!
People ran into the streets in England, too. The weather was cool and drizzly, but the people did not mind. By afternoon the skies had cleared as if even the sun itself were celebrating.

NOT OVER YET
After a few days, the celebrations ended. The war was not over, after all. Thousands of troops were still fighting against Japan. Americans went back to work. War production would continue until all America's troops came home.

The Death of a President

On the minds of many of the celebrators—both in America and England—was one man who had not lived to see victory won. A few weeks earlier, while resting at a health spa in Georgia, President Roosevelt had died of a stroke. Vice President Harry Truman was sworn in as the new leader of the country.

A funeral train carried the president's body from Georgia to Washington. Along the route, hundreds of people stood to watch the train cars pass. Roosevelt had been president for 11 years. One girl remembered, "I thought nobody else would know how to be president."

Roosevelt was buried at his home. A bugler played Taps, then cadets fired rifles three times. After each shot, the president's dog, Fala, barked.

Navy accordionist Graham Jackson had planned to play at a barbecue for Roosevelt on the day he died. Instead, in tears, he played at his funeral.

Surrender in the Pacific

For Americans, the war had begun in the South Pacific, and there it would end. American troops were ready to invade Japan, but everyone knew that millions more lives would be lost. Many people believed they could save lives, both American and Japanese, by using a powerful new top-secret weapon. President Truman and the other Allies finally agreed. On August 6, 1945, an American plane dropped an atomic bomb on the Japanese city of Hiroshima, the headquarters of the Second Japanese Army. Three days later Americans dropped a second atomic bomb on the city of Nagasaki. The destruction was more horrible than anyone had imagined possible. There was no longer a need for an invasion. Japan surrendered.

八月六日 八時 20分頃 皆山小學校より比治山を望む

皆山小學校をあると比治山の内うにきのこ雲があった。先は高いたか

より小さく見えたが見るく大さくなってしまった。ところ

色の煙は何だったのだろうか

AN ATOMIC EXPLOSION
First came a blinding flash of heat and light. Then a violent wind roared across the city. A huge cloud rose into the air. For days, fires raged, purple smoke hung over Hiroshima, and a black rain fell. Thousands died.

A TERRIBLE SIGHT
One man drew this picture from his boyhood memory of the first explosion. "*Going out of an air-raid shelter, I could see the mushroom cloud. The top was narrower than below, but it was getting bigger as I watched.*"

Survivors wandered across the burned city searching for their families.

V-J DAY
At Pearl Harbor, where everything had begun for Americans, navy rockets and searchlights announced victory in Japan. In contrast, hundreds of Japanese gathered before their emperor's palace and wept.

Yasuko's World

Eight-year-old Yasuko Kurachi lived in a city on the west coast of Japan called Kanazawa. She was lucky to be far from the battlegrounds of Hiroshima and Nagasaki, but the war changed her life, too.

Yasuko took on new responsibilities during the war, just as Molly did. She became a neighborhood leader for her school. Younger children lined up behind her, two by two. She made certain they got to school and back again safely. Like Molly, Yasuko played war games, chasing the enemy with sticks. As the war continued, food and clothing became scarce, just as they did in America. Yasuko's mother sold the family's valuables, even her beautiful silk kimonos, for potatoes and rice. She sewed Yasuko a winter coat from an old blanket.

Yasuko knew nothing of the bombs dropped on her country. She first learned that the war had ended by listening to the emperor of her country over the radio. She was not frightened or angry when Japan surrendered. She did not cry as others did. All she felt was relief. Perhaps now her family would have more food and her mother would again be able to wear beautiful silk kimonos.

A MOST CRUEL BOMB
Emperor Hirohito told his people that fighting against the enemy's "new and most cruel bomb" would result in the "extinction of human civilization." The Japanese officially surrendered on September 2, 1945.

Japanese Minister Shigemitsu, left, signed the terms of surrender for the emperor.

STOPPED TIME
At the center of the blast, it was so hot that everything burned, like this watch, which stopped at the moment of the explosion—8:15 in the morning.

A Thousand Cranes

In time, the skies cleared over the Japanese city of Hiroshima. The cherry trees bloomed again in spring. Still, the horror of Hiroshima was hard to forget. Perhaps that was a good thing, for if people remembered, they might prevent such destruction and death from happening again. That was the dream of one little girl from Hiroshima named Sadako Sasaki.

Sadako was just two years old when the atomic bomb destroyed the city where she lived. The blast slammed her against the kitchen wall of her home, but she was not badly hurt. Her country and her people healed. Sadako grew up happy. She ran on her school relay team, and she had many friends. She believed people—all people— were good inside and peace was possible.

One day when she was 12 years old, she became very ill with a disease called *leukemia* (loo-KEE-mee-uh). The cause of her illness was the harmful radiation that had fallen with the rain over Hiroshima after the explosion of the atomic bomb. Sadako faced her illness bravely. She believed in the ancient Japanese legend that cranes can live for 1,000 years. She wanted to live, and the legend gave her hope. Perhaps Japan's birds of peace would protect her if she did something wonderful to honor them.

Sadako knew the Japanese art of *origami*, folding squares of colorful paper into tiny shapes. Now Sadako began to fold little paper cranes. If she could fold 1,000 cranes, then perhaps the graceful birds would save her. Sadako folded 664 paper cranes before she died in October 1955. The children in her school folded the remaining cranes and brought them to her funeral.

The atomic blast had poisoned Sadako's blood, but it could not poison her spirit. Her belief in the goodness of people and her wish for world peace spread from Japan to other countries. All around the world, children began to fold paper cranes and send them to Japan—by the thousands. Sadako's friends raised money to build a Children's Monument for Peace to honor all the children who had been harmed by the atomic bomb. That monument stands today in Peace Park in the heart of Hiroshima. The sculpture shows Sadako on top of a mountain with her arms raised. In her hands is a crane.

Engraved upon the stone are these words:

This is our cry.
This is our prayer.
Peace in the world.

At the foot of the sculpture are millions of origami cranes sent to Hiroshima from children all around the world. As long as there are children who believe in peace, the cranes will continue to come.

Homecomings

Although the war was over, many months passed before all the soldiers returned home. The waiting was hard for children like Molly who had not seen their fathers for two years or more. On the day ten-year-old Larry Calvert's father was to return home, Larry hung an American flag from the limbs of a maple tree in his front yard. Then he sat on the street curb and waited. At lunchtime, his mother brought him a sandwich and a glass of cold milk. At last, a taxicab stopped in front of the house. His father scooped Larry into his arms. Larry felt just what Molly had felt when her father came home and hugged her—joy. Perfect joy.

DO YOU WANT YOUR WIFE TO WORK AFTER THE WAR ?

WAR DEPARTMENT EDUCATION MANUAL EM-31 G I ROUNDTABLE SERIES

GIVE A MAN A JOB
When the soldiers came home, women were asked to leave their jobs to make way for the men. Many hated losing the independence they had worked so hard to gain.

BABY BOOM
Some women were happy to become full-time housewives and mothers again. In fact, so many new babies were born in the years following the war that the country announced a "baby boom"!

QUEEN OF THE ATLANTIC
The *Queen Mary* had taken thousands of troops to war. Now she brought them home. Soldiers crowded the decks as the ship arrived in New York.

In some suburbs, like Levittown, Pennsylvania, all the houses were the same. They were partly built in factories.

THE AMERICAN DREAM

By the late 1940s, a typical American family living in the suburbs had a stay-at-home mom and three children.

SUBURBS

Whole new towns called *suburbs* were built to house America's new families. Suburbs were built just outside of cities. Families relied on cars to take them to work and shop in the city and to go on vacation.

TELEVISION

Factories that had made tanks and planes during the war, started making washing machines, refrigerators, and televisions.

A Peek into the Future

"The war has changed things," said Mrs. McIntire.
"But some things are still the same."

—Meet Molly

★

When World War Two ended, Molly was ten years old. During the years that her father was away, she had learned important lessons about making do with less and caring for others. Now that the war was over, Molly's life changed once again, as did the lives of all Americans.

Some changes were wonderful. Molly's father was home at last. Gone were turnips from the Victory garden and food ration stamps. The McIntire family might have bought a new refrigerator or perhaps even a television set!

Some changes were bittersweet. Each November on Veterans' Day, Molly might have marched in a hometown parade and later placed American flags on the graves of soldiers who had died for the freedom of others around the world.

The most important lesson Molly learned during the war was that she could count on herself—and she could make a difference, whether it was to ensure a happy Christmas holiday or to dance in a school talent show. As Molly grew older in the years following the war, that lesson would have become even more important to her. Although she no longer saved bottle caps or knitted for the Red Cross, Molly would have devoted her time to other important causes. Perhaps she volunteered in the hospital where her father worked. Or, having read about Sadako, she folded paper cranes for peace. And she would have sent them to the Children's Monument in Hiroshima.

In her heart she would know that it was the perfect thing to do.